Major League SOCCER

New York Red Bulls

Joanne Mattern

Mitchell Lane
PUBLISHERS

2001 SW 31st Avenue
Hallandale, FL 33009

www.mitchelllane.com

Mitchell Lane

PUBLISHERS

Printing   1   2   3   4   5   6   7   8

Designer: Ed Morgan
Editor: Sharon F. Doorasamy

Library of Congress Cataloging-in-Publication Data

Names: Mattern, Joanne, 1963– author.
Title: New York Red Bulls / by Joanne Mattern.
Description: Hallandale, FL : Mitchell Lane Publishers, 2019. | Series: Major League Soccer |
    Includes bibliographical references and index.
Identifiers: LCCN 2018003130| ISBN 9781680202526 (library bound) | ISBN 9781680202533 (ebook)
Subjects: LCSH: New York Red Bulls (Soccer team)
Classification: LCC GV943.6.N46 M38 2018 | DDC 796.334/64097471—dc23
LC record available at https://lccn.loc.gov/2018003130

PHOTO CREDITS: Design Elements, freepik.com, Cover Photo: Robert Giroux/Getty Images, p. 5 freepik.com, p. 6 Stephen Dunn/ ALLSPORT/Getty Images, p. 8 freepik.com, p. 11 Simon Bruty /Allspo Getty Images, p. 12 DON EMMERT/AFP/Getty Images) Purchase, p. 14 Mike Stobe/Getty Images, p. 17 freepik.com, p. 18 Mike Stobe/Getty Images, p. 21 Rob Tringali/Getty Images, p. 22 Mike Stobe/Getty Images, p. 23 Bryan Winter /Sports Illustrated/Getty Images, p. 25 Boris Streubel/Bongarts/Getty Images, p. 26 freepik.com, p. 27 Karina Hessland/Bongarts/Getty Images

Contents

Words in **bold** throughout
can be found in the Glossary.

Major League Soccer

Millions of people around the world love soccer. Some people enjoy playing the game. Others love to watch their favorite club in action. Soccer is the most popular sport in the world. More than 240 million people play soccer. Soccer, called football in most places, is played in almost every country in the world.

The rules of soccer are pretty simple. The idea is to kick a ball down the field and into the goal to score a point. Historians believe the modern form of soccer began in England hundreds of years ago. People from Europe brought the game to the United States during the 1850s.

Countries in Europe had football clubs for many years. But the first North American **league** did not begin until 1968. That year, 17 clubs formed the North American Soccer League, or NASL. Many players came from other countries to play in the NASL. However, the NASL made up different rules than other soccer leagues around the world. The league also had money problems. In 1984, the NASL went out of business.

Soccer fans in America could still watch **matches** from other countries. Americans turned their attention to the World Cup. The World Cup is the world's biggest soccer championship. It is run by an organization called Federation Internationale de Football Association, or FIFA. Clubs from all over the world play in the World Cup every four years.

Fans packed the stands during MLS's opening season in 1996. Soccer fans were thrilled to finally have a professional soccer league in the U.S.

The United States wanted to host the World Cup, but FIFA said no because the United States did not have a **professional** soccer league. Finally, in 1994, FIFA said the World Cup could be played in the United States if the United States promised to start a professional league. That league would follow the same rules as all other countries. The United States agreed and Major League Soccer (MLS) was born. The first MLS season was in 1996.

MLS started with 10 clubs. Those clubs were the Colorado Rapids, the Columbus Crew, the Dallas Burn, D.C. United, the Kansas City Wiz, the Los Angeles Galaxy, the New England Revolution, the New York/New Jersey MetroStars, the San Jose Clash, and the Tampa Bay Mutiny.

By 2017, MLS had gotten much bigger. That year, MLS had 22 clubs. Nineteen of the clubs are from the United States. Three of the clubs are in Canada. The clubs are divided into Eastern and Western **conferences**.

In 2017, the Eastern Conference clubs were the Atlanta United FC, the Chicago Fire, the Columbus Crew FC, the D.C. United, the Montreal Impact, the New England Revolution, the New York City FC, the New York Red Bulls, the Orlando City FC, the Philadelphia Union, and the Toronto FC.

The Western Conference clubs included the Colorado Rapids, FC Dallas, the Houston Dynamo, the LA Galaxy, the Minnesota Untied FC, the Portland Timbers, Real Salt Lake, the San Jose Earthquakes, the Seattle Sounders, Sporting Kansas City, and the Vancouver Whitecaps FC.

MLS only includes clubs from the United States and Canada. However, players from all over the world play on these clubs. In 2017, MLS clubs included players from 67 countries. The top five birthplace countries for MLS clubs that year were:

United States	**288 players**
Canada	**28 players**
Argentina	**24 players**
England	**22 players**
Ghana	**16 players**

In 2017, Latin American countries had 115 players in the league. That number included 24 players from Argentina, 14 from Brazil, 13 from Colombia, 13 from Costa Rica, and 10 from Honduras. Other players have joined the league from many different countries in Africa, Europe, and Asia.

Each MLS club has 18 players on its game-day **roster**. These players can take part in that day's match. Other players on the roster do not play in that day's match. A roster can have up to eight players from other countries.

Every year, clubs hold a **draft**. Many talented players are drafted to join the different clubs in the league. Some of these players come from college clubs. Others come from international clubs. Still more come from other soccer clubs in the United States and Canada.

MLS players spend most of the year at work. Players report to training camp in January. At camp they practice their skills. New players and returning players learn to work together.

The MLS season lasts from March to October. There are 34 matches in a season. Twenty-three of those matches are against clubs in the same conference. The other 11 matchs are played against clubs in the other conference.

In November, there is a 12-match **playoff** series called the MLS Cup Playoffs. The top five clubs from each conference compete in the playoffs. Each conference starts with a **knockout round**. After that, a series of **semifinals** and **finals** narrow the competition down to one club from each conference.

Finally, those top two clubs meet in the MLS Cup Championship. The championship match is played in December. The winner of the MLS Cup is awarded the Philip F. Anschutz Trophy. This trophy is named after one of the founders of MLS.

MLS clubs earn points for each win and tie during the season. The club with the most points wins an award called the Supporters' Shield.

MLS clubs can also play in the Canadian Championships and the CONCACAF Champions League. The CONCACAF includes clubs from Mexico, Central America, and Caribbean nations. The winner of the CONCACAF Cup qualifies to play in the World Cup.

Each club in Major League Soccer has a story to tell, including the New York Red Bulls. This club has changed a lot since the early days of MLS.

Fun Facts

1 The first set of soccer rules was created in England in 1815.

2 Why do so many MLS clubs have the initials "FC" in their names? "FC" stands for "football club."

How the Red Bulls Started

CHAPTER TWO

The New York Red Bulls was one of the original MLS clubs when the league started in 1996. However, at that time, the club had a different name. It was called the New York/New Jersey MetroStars.

The MetroStars hired some well-known names to start the club. Tab Ramos was the first player to sign a contract with the club. Ramos had played in the 1994 World Cup. The club's first coach was Eddie Firmani. Firmani had played for the New York Cosmos in the old NASL.

Before they were the Red Bulls, they were the MetroStars. Two MetroStars players, Roberto Donadoni and Nicola Caricola (*right*), talk to a referee during a 1996 game in New Jersey's Giants Stadium.

The MetroStars got off to a rough start. Its first home match was against the New England Revolution. MetroStar Nicola Caricola accidentally kicked the ball into his club's own goal. New England won 1–0. The club ended the season with a 15–17 record. The MetroStars were third in the Eastern Conference and made the playoffs, but they lost to D.C. United.

In 1999, the club had its worst year with a 7–25 record. It was the worst record in MLS history. Things could only get better for the MetroStars—and they did.

In 2000, the MetroStars had their first winning season. They ended up in first place in the Eastern Conference with a 17-12-3 record. The MetroStars made it to the semifinals of both the MLS Playoffs and the U.S. Open Cup. 2001 was another winning season.

Bob Bradley coached the MetroStars between 2003-2005 and led the team to the MLS playoffs.

In 2003, the club got a new manager named Bob Bradley. Bradley led the club to the MLS playoffs and the U.S. Open Cup final that year. In 2004, the MetroStars became the first MLS club to win a trophy outside of North America. They won the La Manga Cup after defeating clubs from the Ukraine and Norway. In 2005, the club made it to the playoffs once again but lost to the New England Revolution.

In 2006, the MetroStars were bought by the energy-drink company Red Bull. The club's name was changed to the New York Red Bulls. Coach Bruce Arena led the Red Bulls to the 2007 MLS playoffs. Once again they lost to the New England Revolution.

The Red Bulls' best season turned out to be 2008. They made it to the finals of the MLS Cup but lost to the Columbus Crew. However, the 2009 season was a disaster. At one point, the club had a 16-match losing streak.

The Red Bulls knew they had to make some big changes for the 2010 season. The new head coach, Hans Backe, signed many European players, including French star Thierry Henry. The Red Bulls won first place in the Eastern Conference. But they lost to the San Jose Earthquakes in the conference semifinals. The 2011 and 2012 seasons were much the same, and Backe was let go.

Mike Petke became head coach in 2012. He pushed the club to be more **aggressive** on the field. The Red Bulls won the 2013 Supporters' Shield with the best record in the MLS. The club also made it to the quarterfinals of the MLS Cup. In 2014, they made it to the Eastern Conference final but lost to the New England Revolution.

Petke was let go at the start of the 2015 season. The Red Bulls won the Supporters' Shield again in 2015 and reached the Eastern Conference final. However, they lost to the Columbus Crew. In 2016, the club made it to the CONCACAF Champions League for the first time.

Another average season was in 2017. As of mid-July, the club was in seventh place in the Eastern Conference with a record of 8-8-2.

When the club was the MetroStars, they wore solid black or solid white **jerseys**. Later they switched to home jerseys that had red and black stripes. Once they became the Red Bulls, the club wore white shirts and red shorts at home, and navy blue and yellow uniforms for away matches.

The club's badge has also changed over the years. The first MetroStars badge featured skyscrapers. Later this changed to a shield with the club's name, red and black stripes, a star, and a soccer ball. When the club became the Red Bulls, the badge featured the club name around two bulls with a soccer ball between them.

The MetroStars played at Giants Stadium in East Rutherford, New Jersey, from 1996 until 2009. In 2010, the Red Bulls began playing at their new stadium, Red Bull Arena. The Arena is located in Harrison, New Jersey.

Red Bull Arena was built specifically to host soccer matches. The stadium holds more than 25,000 fans.

Both Giants Stadium and Red Bull Arena can hold slightly more than 25,000 fans. Attendance was almost 24,000 during the 1996 season but went down sharply after that. In 2009, only 12,229 fans attended home matches. However, attendance has gone up since then. In 2016, the club hosted 20,620 fans during the regular season and 24,314 during the playoffs.

The New York Red Bulls have very loyal fans. The club's first fan club was called the Empire Supporters Club. In 2005, another group of New Jersey fans was formed. It was called the Garden State Supporters. Later, this club became known as the Garden State Ultras. In 2010, another group formed to honor the many **Scandinavian** players on the club. These supporters were called the Viking Army Supporters Club. Each group of supporters has its own section of the stadium where they can sit and cheer on their favorite club.

Fun Facts

1 In 1998, the club dropped "New York/New Jersey" from its name. Now they were simply the MetroStars.

2 The Red Bulls's training center is in Hanover, New Jersey. It has three grass fields and one **turf** field.

Playing Our Game

Each soccer club has 11 players on the field. Usually, four players play **defense**. They protect the goal and try to keep the other club from scoring. Defenders block shots and kick the ball away from the goal.

Four midfielders play both defense and **offense**. When their club is trying to score, they move forward with the ball. When their club is trying to stop the other club, they move back on defense.

Forwards are offensive players. They move the ball forward to the other club's goal. The striker plays down the middle of the field. Wingers play on the sides. They try to feed the ball to the striker so he can score.

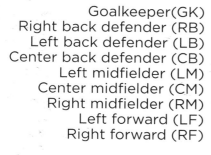

Goalkeeper(GK)
Right back defender (RB)
Left back defender (LB)
Center back defender (CB)
Left midfielder (LM)
Center midfielder (CM)
Right midfielder (RM)
Left forward (LF)
Right forward (RF)

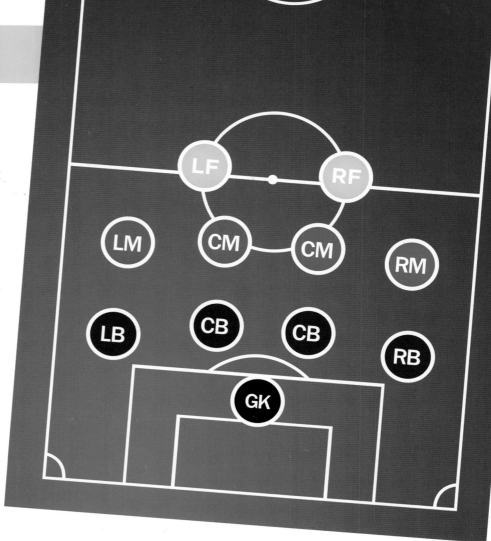

The final player on the club is the goalkeeper. His job is to guard the goal and block shots from the other club. The goalkeeper is the only player who is allowed to use his hands to block a shot or catch the ball.

Mascots are another important part of a soccer club. Even though mascots don't play, they are often on the field to help fans get excited. Mascots also take part in giveaways and contests. They pose for pictures and sign autographs. They also take part in community events. However, not all MLS clubs have a mascot. The New York Red Bulls is one of those clubs. However, the club does sell a stuffed red bull with the club logo on it.

Red Bulls star Juan Pablo Angel (*right*) controls the ball during a 2009 match against D.C. United.

Like all sports clubs, the New York Red Bulls has a **rivalry** with some of the other clubs in the league. The club's main rival is D.C. United. The two clubs have faced off several times in championship matches. The Philadelphia Union are also rivals because the two clubs' home cities are fairly close to each other.

The Red Bulls also have a strong rivalry with the New England Revolution. Many New York and New England clubs are rivals. The rivalry became even stronger after the Revolution had a 20-match undefeated streak against the Red Bulls.

In 2015, another New York club joined MLS. This club was the New York City FC. The FC and the Red Bulls quickly became rivals. Their fans even fought with each other during matches. The rivalry between the Red Bulls and the FC became known as the Hudson River Derby.

Whether two clubs are rivals or just opponents, it can be a challenge to play a match on the other club's home field. Playing at home often means the stands are full of your club's fans. These fans support the club by cheering, waving signs, and other actions. However, when a club plays at an opponent's stadium, the fans are there to cheer for the other club. Often, fans will shout at the visiting club and try to distract players from the match.

Another reason playing on another club's field can be difficult is the club is not familiar with it. Although soccer fields are standard, each stadium has its own features. Other factors, such as weather or altitude, can make things hard for a visiting club.

Fun Fact

The Revolution's winning streak against the Red Bulls lasted for 12 years.

The Red Bulls's Best Players

The New York Red Bulls have been around for more than 20 years. During that time, the club has seen some amazing players. Here are some of the club's all-time stars:

Tab Ramos (1996–2002)

Ramos was born in Uruguay but moved to the United States when he was 11 years old. He was the first player drafted in the MLS in 1995 but played for a year in Mexico. The MLS clubs were not ready to play yet. In 1996, he was transferred to the MetroStars and played for seven seasons. In 2002, he retired from soccer with a record of eight goals and 36 **assists**.

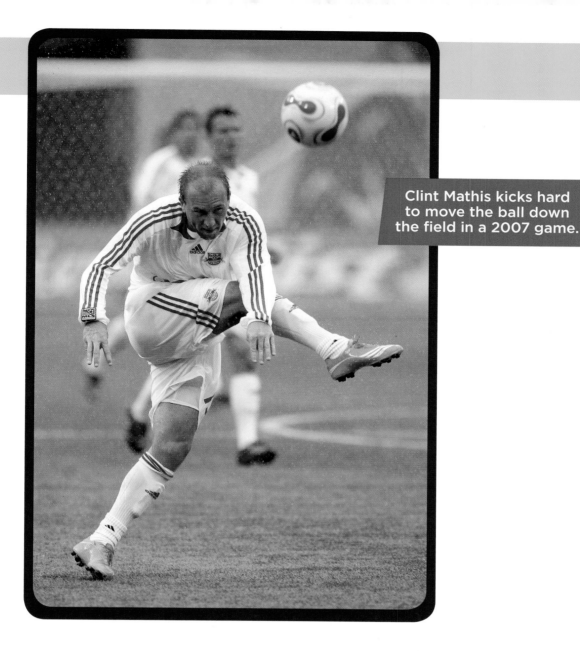

Mike Amman (1999–2000)

Although he only played two seasons with the Red Bulls, Amman is one of the club's best goalkeepers. He achieved 199 saves in 46 matches. Amman was named Club Defender of the Year during both seasons.

Clint Mathis (2000–2003, 2007)

Clint Mathis is best known for scoring five goals in one match in 2000. Playing both as a forward and a midfielder, he scored 39 goals during his years with the Red Bulls, with 10 of those goals being match winners.

Chapter Four

Juan Pablo Angel (2007-2010)

Playing at forward, Angel was named MLS Player of the Week and MLS Player of the Month after he made his **debut** with the Red Bulls in 2007. He also became the first Red Bull player to score in six straight matches. He led the club in scoring between 2007–2009 and helped the club win its second Eastern Conference title.

Thierry Henry (2010-2014)

French player Henry was an international star for many years before coming to the Red Bulls as a striker in 2010. His career highlights include a goal and two assists against the Chicago Fire in the last match of the 2013 season. That win gave the Red Bulls the regular-season championship for the first time. In July 2014, Henry scored a goal and three assists in a match against the Columbus Crew and became the Red Bulls's all-time assist leader. Henry retired after the 2014 season.

Thierry Henry (*left*) shows why he is one of the Red Bulls's best and most famous players with this skillful move.

Head's up! Sacha Kljestan (*center*) defies gravity to head a ball during a match against the New England Revolution.

Sacha Kljestan (2015-2017)

This former member of the U.S. Olympic team played for several European clubs before joining the Red Bulls as a midfielder in 2015. His ability to score goals helped the Red Bulls win many matches and advance in the 2015 U.S. Open Cup playoffs and the 2016 CONCACAF Champions League. Kljestan is also great at assists. In October of 2016, he became only the second MLS player to reach 20 assists in a season. In 2017, Kljestan became the Red Bulls club captain. However, at the start of the 2018 season, the club traded Kljestan to the Orlando City FC and named goalkeeper Luis Robles as their new captain.

Communicating On and Off the Field

CHAPTER FIVE

Soccer is an international sport with players in almost every country on Earth. Although MLS is based in English-speaking North America, MLS clubs have players from many different nations. These players may speak many different languages other than English.

At the start of the 2017 season, the New York Red Bulls had 26 active players on its roster. Fourteen of these players were from the United States. The other players were from 11 foreign countries. Two players were from France and two were from Cameroon. The other players were from Haiti, Brazil, Argentina, Panama, Austria, Jamaica, England, and Ghana.

Communication is key in soccer, as in any sport. Players have come up with many different ways to talk to each other on and off the field. Communication is not as difficult as you might think. Players who understand the match do not need words to communicate with each other on the field. They just know how to read signals to understand what they should do. A player's body language also can tell other players what he plans to do and how they should react.

Words aren't always needed in soccer. Marcel Sabitzer signals to his Red Bull teammates during a match.

Many soccer athletes travel from one county to another during their time playing the match. Along the way, these players pick up important words and phrases in their new language. Of course, they learn important soccer words and directions. Many international players learn English in school. This is especially true in Europe and Africa.

No matter what language a player speaks, it can be difficult to adjust to playing in a different country. Many things in the United States are different from other nations. The United States is a very large country, so foreign players have to get used to increased travel time. Weather conditions can also change. A club may play in snow or ice one week. The next week may see them playing in a hot, humid climate.

No matter what language they speak, teammates and coaches have a strong bond. They help each other and work together. All the players on the Red Bulls want the same thing. They want to win!

Daniel Frahn reacts to receiving a yellow card penalty from referee Patrick Ittrich.

Fun Facts

1 Cards can also bridge the language barrier. **Referees** use different colored cards to warn players about **penalties**. Yellow cards warn the player that he has done something wrong. Red cards mean the player has to leave the field.

2 **Altitude** can also affect soccer players. Some clubs are high above sea level. The air is thinner than it is in a stadium that has a lower altitude. Thinner air can make it hard for players to breathe, and it can even make them feel sick.

What You Should Know

- The name MetroStars came from a company called Metromedia. Metromedia was owned by John Kluge. Kluge was also one of the owners of the MetroStars.

- The Empire Supporters Club formed in 1995, before the club played its first match.

- In 1996, the Metro Stars announced they had drafted players named Juninho and Tulio. Excited fans thought the club had signed the famous Brazilian players Juninho Paulista and Tulio Costa. However, the real identities of the players remained a mystery, and they never joined the club.

- On August 26, 2000, MetroStar Clint Mathis set an MLS record by scoring five goals in one match.

- On August 18, 2007, the Red Bulls hosted the LA Galaxy and their new star, David Beckham. A crowd of 66,238 fans attended the match, setting an MLS record.

- The Red Bulls are the only MLS club that has not won a major championship.

- The Red Bulls had 16 head coaches between 1996 and 2017.

- The New York Red Bulls Academy trains young soccer players in the New York area. Players pay nothing to be part of the program.

2016–2017 Quick Stats

35 games played	40 winning percentage
13 wins	411 shots taken
5 draws	201 shots on target
14 losses	64 goals scored

1996
The **New York/New Jersey MetroStars** are named as one of MLS original clubs.

1998
"New York/New Jersey" is dropped from the club's name.

1999
The **MetroStars** have the worst record in MLS history.

2000
The **MetroStars** have their first winning season; Clint Mathis scores five goals in one game, an MLS record.

2006
The team's name is changed to the New York Red Bulls.

2008
The Red Bulls have their best season and advance to the MLS Cup Finals.

2013
The team wins the Supporters' Shield for the first time.

2015
The Red Bulls win the Supporters' Shield for the second time.

Glossary

aggressive
Ready to attack

altitude
Distance above sea level

assists
Helping another player score a goal

conferences
Groups of sports clubs within a league

debut
First appearance in a game

defense
Players who try to keep the other club from scoring in a match

draft
To choose young players to join a sports league

finals
The playoff round that determines which clubs will face each other in the championship

jerseys
Shirts worn by a player on a sports club

knockout round
The playoff round that determines which clubs move on to the semifinals

league
A groups of sports clubs that play each other

mascots
People or animals that symbolize a club

matches
Soccer games

offense
Players who try to score in a match

penalties
Punishments given to players or a club for breaking rules

playoff
A match to determine which clubs will go on to the championship

professional
Doing something for money rather than as a hobby

referees
People who enforce the rules during a match

rivalry
Intense competition between two clubs

roster
A list of players on an MLS club

Scandinavian
Having to do with the countries of Norway, Sweden, Denmark, Finland, and Iceland

semifinals
The playoff round that determines which clubs move on to the finals

turf
Artificial grass

Further Reading

Kortemeier, Todd. *Total Soccer*. Minneapolis, MN: Abdo Publishing, 2017.

Laughlin, Kara L. *Soccer*. Mankato, MN: The Child's World, 2016.

Rausch, David. *Major League Soccer*. Minneapolis, MN: Bellwether Media, 2015.

On the Internet

Get Active with MLS
http://getactivewithmls.com/kids

MLS Soccer
http://www.mlssoccer.com

New York Red Bulls
http://www.newyorkredbulls.com

New York Red Bulls Facts for Kids
https://wiki.kidzsearch.com/wiki/New_York_Red_Bulls

Index

About the Author

Joanne Mattern is the author of many books for children on a variety of subjects, including sports, history, and biography. She has written many books for Mitchell Lane. Joanne loves to learn about people, places, and events and bring historical figures to life for today's readers. She lives in New York State with her husband, children, and several pets.